Jan & [heart]
Best Wishes!

Jas Swedberg

Ps. 90:17

Lessons from a Mama's Boy

...How Mom Taught Me
to Be a Success
in Business
and Life

Milestone Books, Inc.
Author Services Division
~changing lives one book at a time~
getpublished@milestonebooks.net

Printed and bound in the United States of America

Acknowledgments

I could easily fill pages and pages with people who have helped me and need to be thanked. First, thank you to the most wonderful mom in the world. She taught me so much and is one of my greatest fans. Thank you to my dad for teaching me how to be a good husband, father, man and so much more. He's one of those hard workers who is always in the background.

Thank you to my siblings, Steve, Stacy, Shaun and Stephanie (Mom liked names that started with S), who all helped keep their big brother grounded and laughing.

Thank you to very special friends. Andrea Nierenberg and Gary Fenton have been my mentors throughout this entire process and have taught me so much. Jim Blasingame has been my wise sage. Lisa Merizio-Smith has been a cheerleader. My two best friends, Doug Lackey and Bill McCann, have encouraged me from day one when I said I wanted to write a book.

However, none of this would have been possible without the love, support and encouragement of Kathie - my wife, best buddy and biggest fan. I also want to thank my two boys, Jake and Matt, who loved the idea.

Lastly and most importantly, I want to thank God for bringing these people and many others into my life. He has blessed me in so many ways.

Lessons from a Mama's Boy

...How Mom Taught Me
to Be a Success
in Business
and Life

Table of Contents

Table of Contents

Section 3: Actions

Last Thought

Introduction

Who taught you to walk, wipe your nose, tie your shoes and clean behind your ears? Much of your success in life today can be traced back to the valuable advice your mother gave you - don't run with scissors; don't cross your eyes, they'll stick that way; eat all your vegetables, there are children starving in India. Well, maybe not all the things she told you, but most of it. Moms have a unique way of teaching lessons that last a lifetime.

How many of you wished you would have listened to your mother more? Okay, here's your chance.

Every organization and individual wants to be more successful and is willing to spend a lot of money to do so. You might have tried several different approaches to finding success, but just can't seem to get it right. You may have attended seminars and read books promoting success. Books like *Leadership Secrets of Attila the Hun* promote an attacking, winner-take all approach; while *Who Moved My Cheese* has a softer approach. Yet there still seems to be something missing.

Then I thought of my mom. She is one of the most successful people in the world. What were the lessons she had taught me about success?

I have been very blessed to have many wonderful influences in my life with my parents standing out above them all. Mom and Dad, each in their own unique way, taught me many powerful life lessons, which have greatly contributed to my success - a success that has been more than just money or titles. I have been blessed with an awesome wife, loving family, great friends, opportunities to give back and so much more.

But enough about me, let's talk about Mom. Shirley Durham grew up in East Hanover, New Jersey, a small community not far outside of New York City. She graduated from high school in 1954. Three years later she married my dad, moved to a foreign country (Mississippi), and started a family. After fifty years of marriage, five children and twelve grandchildren, she is just getting better all the time.

Mom never attended college, took a class or read anything on marketing or success. Yet her life has been a phenomenal success. As a marketing genius, she has succeeded at selling all her life. Every day she's spending time in her market learning all she can in order to better serve her customers.

Any organization or individual looking to increase their influence and value in the marketplace, or in life, will want to incorporate her philosophies. She is successful in every sense of the word and you will be too if you follow these proven ideas.

Section 1

Circle

of

Friends

In the movie *Tombstone*, Val Kilmer plays the part of Doc Holiday, a character who does not endear himself to many people. During a scene toward the end of the movie, another cowboy named Jack asks Doc Holiday why he's risking his life to help Wyatt Earp. The conversation goes like this:

>Jack: **Why are you here, Doc?**
>
>Doc Holiday: **Wyatt's my friend.**
>
>Jack: **Heck, I've got lots of friends.**
>
>Doc Holiday: **Well I don't.**

Doc Holiday's words give us clear insight into the importance of friends. Cowboy Jack took his friends for granted. Doc, on the other hand, cherished the one true friend he had. This recognition of the importance of friends is the cornerstone to my mom's success. She treats every friend as if they're **the only one she has.**

It never fails when I'm home visiting that I meet someone who tells me they know my mom and how much they love her. These are people of all ages, races, and walks of life who have become friends with my mom. I always thank them for their kind words and ask how they met her. Their answer is almost always the same:

>*Your mother walked up to me, said "hello,"*
>*asked me my name and complimented me.*

That scenario has been repeated many times over as the start to a life-long friendship with my mom.

How do friends impact your success? Over the next several pages, let's take an assessment to see if you are friend worthy.

Lesson 1

Customers

or

Friends

The only way to have a friend is to be one.

~ *Ralph Waldo Emerson*~

Mom could be the top salesperson in any organization. She is constantly doing market research, asking questions, listening to her customers, putting their needs first, willing to ask for the sale and has a near 100 percent closing rate. Have you guessed what she's selling yet?

That's right. Mom's offering her friendship to the world. She doesn't have customers or prospects. Mom has friends, and lots of them!

You might be thinking of the old used-car salesman stereotype, someone who is constantly promoting themselves. Just the opposite, Mom is *genuinely interested* in the other person and their needs. The only benefit Mom has ever received from her friends is the joy that comes from being a friend and helping that person when they're in need. Because of this, she has more friends than anyone I know.

Mom loves people, which equates to her ability to make friends easily. Everyone Mom comes in contact with is a potential friend.

You too will be much more successful when you begin to look at customers and coworkers as friends. Think about how you feel when a good friend calls. Do you feel the same way when a customer or coworker calls? Or do you dread those calls? When you start treating customers and coworkers the way you would a friend, your whole attitude changes and you actually look forward to helping them.

Too many people today have the exact opposite approach. They treat their friends like customers. Friends are selected based on what can be gained, not given. We want the friend who has great business connections, a house at the beach, tickets to your favorite sports team or gives great parties. Friends are viewed as someone who can take me to my next goal.

A true friend is someone who likes you for who you are as a person. It's not for the job you have, the car you drive or the house you own. I've had associates at Wal-Mart, waitresses, and lawyers alike tell me how nice my mom was to them and how interested she was in their lives.

Mom and Dad live on a farm. So, almost every day Mom travels to one of the surrounding towns. Her purpose is not to shop, but walk the stores and mall seeing friends and meeting new ones. Mom likes to eat at several restaurants in the area, because she knows that's where she will find her customers. In our hometown, she has friends from every walk of life: professionals, waitresses, lawyers, bank executives, sales clerks and many others. Because she treats everyone like a friend, people really like my mom.

Studies have proven that in selling situations if the price is the same we prefer to buy from someone we like – our friends. The same studies also show that even if the price is higher we still prefer to buy from someone we like – our friends.

Think of the people at work and your customers. How many of your coworkers and customers do you consider friends? An even better question is how many of them do you *treat* like a friend? Would they consider you a friend? The really successful people in life are those with the most friends.

There's a very successful Mexican restaurant where our family loves to eat. The food is good but what really makes it such a success are the owners. They stop at every table to meet new customers or say hello to repeat customers. I always thought I was someone really special when they would stop at my table to thank me for coming and ask how I was doing. Then I noticed they did the same thing at every table. Hmmm....

That's what makes their restaurant so successful – they make everyone feel special! The same way you would make a friend feel when eating at your home.

The owners of this restaurant spend a lot of time becoming friends with their customers. You can see the result of their efforts by the number of people willing to wait in line for a table when there are plenty of Mexican and other restaurants nearby without a wait.

Who's waiting in line to do business with your organization? Start treating your customers like friends and watch your line grow.

Homework Lessons for Success

1. Look at all the touch points your organization has with customers. Ask yourself if this is how you would treat a friend. Would you leave a friend on hold for several minutes or at all? Would you ask a friend to fill out a two page application to do business with you? Would you tell a friend you only take cash?

2. Are you adding new friends to your life, or are you like some people who think they have enough friends? You can never have too many friends. It's fine to have one or two best friends, but never stop adding to your group of friends.

3. No matter how many friends you have, don't take any of them for granted. Follow Doc Holiday's example and treat your friends like they're the only one you have in the world.

Lesson 2

Getting

to

Know You

A good listener is not only popular everywhere,
but after a while gets to know something.

~*Wilson Mizner*~

A large part of Mom's success is based on the knowledge she has of her friends. Mom gets no greater joy than talking with people and learning all about their lives. She knows everything about her friends. The business world would call this market research.

Mom will often tell me about things going on in one of her friends' life - like becoming a grandparent. Then she proceeds to ask me if I remember her friend. When I respond "no," Mom reminds me that I met her friend at a birthday party when I was five.

I know it's hard to believe, but there were no PDAs in 1964 and I was more interested in eating cake and pinning a tail on the donkey. Mom however knows the things that are important to her friends and much more.

And it's this knowledge that allows her to meet the needs of her friends. If you know everything about your customers' lives, you will be better able to meet their needs.

So what's her secret? Mom asks questions. Then, most importantly, she listens.

Do you listen or is your first impulse to tell the other person everything about your fascinating life? A person will ask us one question and we're off and running with our life's story. We can't wait to start talking about ourselves: where *I* work, where *I'm* from, where *I* went to school, *my* favorite team, hobby, sport, etc. Notice a common denominator? All those topics have either *I* or *my*.

If you're going to be successful, you have to put aside *I* and become more interested in the other person's life.

People will tell my mom just about anything because she listens and is genuinely interested in them. It's almost scary what people who just met my mom will tell her about their life. The reason is they feel comfortable and safe around her and therefore open up.

How many of you went to "spend the night" parties as a kid? A group of boys would camp out in the backyard and the girls would do who knows what. I don't really know what girls did since I was never invited to a slumber party. I did hear something about making s'mores and painting toenails. I do know both groups would stay up all night sharing their inner-most secrets. Guys would talk about favorite sports team, superheroes, television shows and the girls you either liked or didn't like.

Sitting around the fire, you felt comfortable and safe. You would open up and proudly tell your friends you liked Susie, even if girls *did* have cooties. You really got to know each other and became close friends.

That's one of the keys to being a successful organization or individual – having sleepovers. No, not really, but *knowing all you can about your customers* is. Do you know your customers and prospects the way you know your friends? You can. It just takes a little work.

When businesses and individuals don't know their customers the way they should, it can negatively affect both parties. Not knowing your customers impacts the bottom line. Most of your sales efforts and marketing dollars are wasted, because you're sending the wrong message. Radio and television ads are just noise. Direct mail is junk mail. Emails are spam.

Your customers and prospects are also frustrated because their real wants and desires are not being met. People love *buying* things they really want, but no one wants to be *sold* anything. This same concept applies if you're with a nonprofit organization and how you treat your donors.

I am not supposed to mention Kathie's age, but recently my amazingly beautiful wife had one of those significant milestones in her life. Her birthday also triggered an abundance of direct mail from different organizations. Their offers included many valuable products and services at discounted prices. It sounded great, except for one BIG problem. They were trying to sell their products to "seniors."

Kathie is a lot of things, but senior is not one of them. She doesn't look or feel her age, and the last thing she's going to open is an envelope touting "Senior Benefits." Kathie would rather pay more for a product or service than get a discount from being labeled a senior.

These organizations really don't understand Kathie or the rest of her generation. Kathie is part of one of the largest segments of the U.S. market, baby boomers. Kathie and the rest of the baby boomer generation want to look, think and act young for as long as possible. And they are willing to pay handsomely for that opportunity. We don't want to be lumped into our parents' generation. They're the seniors in our world, not you and me.

A company recently sent me a very impressive mailing promoting their branded credit card. The card offered a very competitive rate and lucrative rewards program, which allowed customers to earn points for valuable products. The problem was not the design of the mailing, the letter, or even the lucrative offer. It was me. I was the problem. They sent the mailing to the wrong person.

The valuable products offered in their rewards program were industrial tools. I barely know how to use a screwdriver, so a hydraulic jack would not be my first choice of something to get for the home or office. However, it's probably the perfect credit card for an auto mechanic, farmer or construction contractor, but it's just another piece of junk mail to me.

You know what I mean. Think of the emails you get. Do you really need a stock tip, another mortgage or a pill of any color? These are all spam because they didn't care to learn what you might actually want.

How can you be more like my mom? Learn everything you can about your customers. Sorry, I mean *friends.*

When I say Mom knows her friends, I mean she knows *everything* about them: names of their spouse, children and grandchildren, where they work, the church they attend, who's having a baby and so on. She asks and they tell her.

If you sell to businesses, become an expert on their industry. Learn all you can about their competitors, goals, trends, technology, and challenges - both internal and external. Become a resource for your customers by bringing them ideas to grow their business or save money. If your customers have a problem, they will automatically think of you as someone who will listen to them and help find a solution to their problem.

Do the same thing with your *contacts* at the business. Become an expert on *their* life. Learn all you can about their job, fellow employees, hobbies, interests, spouse, family, favorite sports team. When you walk into their office, take inventory. It will tell you a lot about the person. What's on their wall and desk? Pictures of family, golf trips or famous people, awards or trophies or sport memorabilia.

This is a little harder to do if you sell to consumers, but it can still be done. Learn all you can about the different customers you serve. What are the demographics of your best customer? Age, gender, income level, marital status, and race are just a few of the things to help you understand your customers and their needs.

Next, understand what your customers buy and why. Wal-Mart's product offerings vary by store based on the purchasing habits of the customers in that area. Snow chains are not offered in Florida. By watching the purchasing habits at every store, they can increase or decrease the quantity of any product going to that store.

Wal-Mart also understands why most customers buy from them: selection and price. At Wal-Mart, you can find almost anything you want at a low price. When we think of Wal-Mart, we think of "Everyday low prices".

Your customers may not be driven by price. There are hundreds of places to get a cup of coffee for less than what you will pay at Starbucks. Yet price is not the driver for Starbucks' customers. They want the unique experience found at Starbucks and don't mind paying for it. One of the reasons I chose my bank was because it had internet banking and branches near my home and work. Convenience is important to me.

You may be thinking your company sells to thousands of customers, so how could you possibly know your customers the way Mom know hers? Amazon.com comes to mind. When you go online to Amazon's website, they know every book you've ever purchased from them and offer several suggestions on books you might like based on your buying history. That's getting to know your customer.

It's time to invite your customers to a sleepover, eat some s'mores and get to know them!

Homework Lessons for Success

1. Treat your customers like friends. Learn all you can about them. Then use that information to make their lives better.

2. It's important to know everyone at an organization. Too often we spend all of our time trying to get to know the CEO when the Executive Assistant has the real power. Everyone who interviews at our company is judged by how they treat our receptionist.

3. How do you learn more about your customers? Ask questions. Then listen, listen, listen!

Lesson 3

Little Black Book

The most valuable commodity I know of is information.

~ from the movie Wall Street~

Once you've learned all this information about your customers, you have to be able to access the information and use it. Mom keeps a lot of the information about her friends in her head. Spouse's and children's names are all in her head. She does keep her friends' mailing addresses in a spiral notebook and their phone numbers on scraps of paper by the phone.

A few years ago for Christmas, we got Mom a small rolodex to put by her phone. Then Kathie took all the scraps of paper and made an address card for each to put in the rolodex. On our next trip home, there were new scraps of paper by the phone and not a single new card added to the rolodex. As far as we could tell, the rolodex had not been used and Mom's old system was back.

As successful as she's been, this is not the "little black book" I would recommend for most people or organizations. Mom found a system that works very well for her and she's sticking to it. I recommend you do the same for yourself. Spend some time researching the best solution for you. Then start collecting all the information you can on your customers and friends.

Many large companies have some type of customer tracking system. There are a number of Customer Relationship

Management (CRM) software tools available based on your unique needs. Whether you follow my mom's approach of keeping all that information in your head, spiral notebooks and on little scraps of paper or not, the important thing is to find the system that works best for you.

Several years ago I walked into The Cavalier Shop, a men's clothing store in Calhoun City, Mississippi - not exactly 5th Avenue or Rodeo Drive. While I had heard a lot about the clothes, this was my first visit to such a fine haberdashery.

The owner immediately introduced himself and asked my name. He then gave me a Coke, one of the small 6 ounce bottles which had been cooling in an old red Coca Cola ice box. What a great marketing approach! He immediately made me feel comfortable and allowed me to reminisce about getting bottled cokes from similar coolers as a kid. We will talk more about this approach later.

He then invited me to look around and left the room. After giving me several minutes to look around, he reappeared and asked if I'm related to Stephanie or Stacy Swedenburg, who happen to be my sister and brother. He shared how both of them had purchased clothes from him and the dates they were last in his store.

He had immediately created credibility and removed any concerns I might have had.

Then he asked if I had attended Mississippi State University like my siblings and if I was in a particular fraternity. The answer to both questions was yes. While helping me try on a jacket, he asked me if I knew several other people who had attended MSU and were in the same fraternity. You guessed it. They too had shopped at his store.

After gathering bits of information, he would again disappear to the backroom. This scenario was repeated over and over again with the same result each time. He was learning about me and reinforcing my decision to shop at his store by relating the experiences of all my friends and family who had also bought clothes there. I spent a lot of money at his store that day.

You are probably asking what he was doing when he would disappear to the back room. Well, I had that same question. He keeps index cards of everyone who has ever shopped at his store and every card was full of information about his customers. I'm still not sure how he cross referenced all that information. But the system worked very well for him and his clothing business.

Before Harvey McKay became a famous author and public speaker, one of the ways he sold the publisher on his first book idea was his network of contacts. At that time, he had multiple rolodexes filled with names and everything there was to know about the person on the card. McKay told the publisher he already had a market for the book, referring to everyone in his rolodex.

Networking experts like Andrea Nierenberg and Keith Farezzo all preach the importance of knowing all you can about your customers, prospects and friends in order to be a resource for them. This is another reason it's important to have a "little black book." When a customer calls with a problem, you will have the answer or know someone who does. My "little black book" allows me to help friends connect with others, solve problems, find jobs and find new employees. But I don't help friends find dates. Sorry!

You see where I'm going with this. I have become a clearinghouse for information. Customers depend on me for all types of information which I keep in Outlook on my laptop and on my Blackberry. No matter where I am, I have all this valuable information at my finger tips.

How well are *you* keeping up with *your* friends?

Homework Lessons for Success

1. Develop a system to keep up with all the information about your friends, family and customers. Spiral notebooks, index cards or a Blackberry - whatever works best for you.

2. Guard this information with your life. There have been numerous stories in the news about stolen identities. This information is priceless, so keep it safe.

3. Keep this information with you at all times. While traveling, I am always getting calls from customers and friends needing help and my Blackberry is the first place I turn.

Lesson 4

Show

the

Love

To love is to receive a glimpse of heaven.

~Karen Sunde~

If you don't like to be kissed, hugged and feel loved, you need to avoid my mom's house. From the moment Mom greets you at the door till you're driving away, she is constantly kissing, hugging and telling you how much she likes you.

In the case of her children and grandchildren, she's telling us how much she loves us. Just as their father before them, my teenage boys have adjusted and might even admit they like having their grandmother hug and kiss them.

Last Christmas, my brother who lives in Atlanta invited a lady he'd been dating and her teenage daughter to our family gathering. You can imagine how hard that could be for his girlfriend, but no words can possibly describe what her 15-year-old daughter was expecting. Deliverance meets Christmas Vacation - we're going to visit Uncle Eddie's family in Mississippi.

When they walked in the door, Mom hugged them both and said how excited she was to have them for Christmas. For the next four days, Mom and the rest of our family loved them like they had always been a part of our family. We exposed them to rural life: deer hunting, riding horses and four wheelers, feeding goats, and so much more. After returning home, the 15-year-old told her mother she couldn't wait to go back next year.

Mom has always understood that in order for any relationship to reach its full potential and last, both parties have to feel loved. In the case of a husband and wife, sometimes husbands don't say "I love you" as much as they should. These men take for granted their wives know how they feel, and never see the need to tell them. There's an old adage that applies here – "You better tell your wife how much you love her before someone else does."

Are you telling your customers how much you love them? Don't assume they know how you feel about having them as a customer. The old adage also applies to your business – You better tell you customer how much you love them before someone else does.

Think of all the things a wife might like and apply it to your customers.

- Anniversary gift – Show your customers you know when they started doing business with your organization and thank them for their years of loyalty.

- Birthday card – Recognize your customer on their special day.

- Flowers and chocolates – Take your customer cookies, donuts, tickets, etc. Show them how much you appreciate their business.

- Dating – Take your customers out for lunch. Get them away from the office.

- Talk and most importantly, listen – Ask your customers what kind of day they've had. These talks are not about you and your product/service, but learning about the customer's challenges and how you can make their life easier.

I am constantly looking for creative ways to let Kathie, my wife, know how much I love her. A few years ago, we were remodeling and landscaping our home, which included painting the outside of the house. The painters were scheduled to start a few days after Valentine's Day.

I had the idea to spray paint the front of my house with "I LOVE YOU," a big heart and XOXOXO for Valentine's Day. Early that morning, I completed the task. When Kathie returned from taking the boys to school, she saw how I felt about her sprayed across the front of our house.

The message achieved its goal and I was a big hit at home for several days. Now the rest of the story – this expression of my feelings for Kathie lasted longer than expected. Due to weather and other issues, our house did not get painted until May. My feelings for Kathie became a big hit with our neighbors and friends. However, Kathie's appreciation for my act of love waned after about a week.

Find ways to let your customers know how much you appreciate their business – just don't spray paint their office.

Homework Lessons for Success

1. You may not be able to hug and kiss your customers, but you can still find ways to show how much you love their business. It needs to be in words and deeds.

2. Be creative. Anyone can order a gift basket or some golf balls for their customer. Show your customer you put some thought into what you're giving them. The dollar amount of the gift is not that important. Think of some of the most cherished gifts you've received. I bet many of them were not very expensive, but it was that the person cared enough to remember you.

3. Everyone likes to feel loved and appreciated. Start with those closest to you - your spouse, children, parents, family members, friends, the people who work for and with you - and tell them how much you love and appreciate them.

Section 2

Attitude

The problem is not the problem. The problem is your attitude about the problem.

~ from *Sisterhood of the Traveling Pants*~

Your attitude has an enormous impact on your success. How you approach your friends, work, family and life are all influenced by your attitude. Don't fret, because here's good news – you can choose your attitude! You're not born with a good or bad attitude. You didn't inherit your attitude from Uncle Joe or anyone else in your family.

Here's another insight. Your attitude has nothing to do with the side of the bed you get up on. Every day you decide what your attitude will be toward others and toward life.

My mom's attitudes have directly contributed to her success in life. I've tried to take a similar approach to hers and hope it shows in how I approach relationships, work and life. You would make Mom very proud if she saw these same attitudes in you. Plus, you would be well on your way to being a success.

Lesson 5

Laughter

The most wasted of all days is one without laughter.

~ ee cummings~

The more you enjoy life, the more enjoyable it will be for the people around you. Because my mom enjoys life and is able to see the humor in things, people love being around her. If you're with her, it's not long before the two of you will be laughing.

Mom has the enviable gift of being able to laugh at herself, as you will see in one of her adventures in life. Every year Mom goes on a trip with her friends to exotic destinations like Pigeon Forge, Tennessee. Three days of meals at Cracker Barrel and shopping at outlet malls sounds too good to be true. And the funny thing is Mom doesn't even like shopping. She prefers to sit outside the stores and talk to everyone while her friends shop.

On past trips, her friends were always complaining about Mom's nightly ritual of washing her undergarments and hanging them in the shower to dry before packing them away. The first night of this trip was no different. On the next night, mom goes through her normal routine in the bathroom and leaves when she's finished. As the next lady takes her turn in the bathroom, she starts laughing hysterically. In place of the normal white grandma panties was a tiny black thong hanging in the shower.

Just one of the many reasons Mom always gets invited on these trips.

So many companies and individuals have forgotten how to have fun...how to laugh. Southwest Airlines hasn't. If you've ever flown with them, you know their pilots and flight attendants make the trip fun. You might hear a joke, a song or something to make you laugh. You won't see an unenthused flight attendant repeating the same boring message before every flight. I actually listen and watch them putting the oxygen mask over their face to see what they might do.

This fun attitude makes Southwest Airlines different in the airline industry and I believe is one of the reasons Southwest has been so successful. As I'm writing this, the Southwest flight attendant is singing a version of "She'll Be Coming Round the Mountain" to encourage us to pick up trash and put away our tray tables.

Tom Whaley knows the importance of fun. He is the Executive Vice President with the St. Paul Saints, minor league baseball team, and has been extremely successful in filling their 6,000 seat stadium. In an interview in *Fast Company*, Tom shared "We play in this ramshackle municipal park by the tracks with aluminum bleachers on concrete. If we just did baseball, we'd probably have 1,000 people here a night. If you look back over 13 seasons, we have averaged 90% capacity, and last year we had higher revenues than ever, and I credit that to fun."

Tom continues "We put a lot of work into having fun and trying to come up with stuff that makes us laugh or causes conversation. We try to move fast and react to the news. The day after Commissioner Bud Selig had called a tie at the All-Star game, we were all talking about it. I mean, baseball is the one game you can't end in a tie. So the guy who's doing our merchandise says, 'Let's do Bud Selig Tie Night.' And in six hours we got the whole thing together. We had the ties purchased and silk-screened. It was even on ESPN.com by 3 p.m., and it was only an idea at 8 a.m. in the morning. The funny thing is, we never played the game. It got rained out."

Like Mom, laughter and fun is an important part of my life and work. If you ever get my voice mail at work, you'll never hear "I am currently on the other line" or "I am away from the phone, please leave a message." My messages will hopefully make you laugh or at least smile. The same is true of my away-from-the-office email messages.

Two examples of past voice mail messages are "Hello, you've reached Scott Swedenburg. I am sitting at my desk and not on the phone. However, I am daydreaming of marketing ideas to grow your business and can't answer the phone. Leave your name and number so we can start growing your business as soon as possible." Another is "Hello, you've reached Scott Swedenburg. St. Patrick's Day is just around the corner. If you want to find your pot of gold, don't wait on leprechauns to leave it at the end of a rainbow. Let us grow your business using direct marketing. Please leave your name and number and make your competitors green with envy."

Does this approach work? My experience has definitely been yes. I am constantly having customers, prospects and vendors leave me a voice mail saying how much they loved my message and how it made them laugh. Depending on the quality of my message, I might answer the phone only to have someone ask to be put into my voicemail so their office can listen to my message.

Recently, I had two voicemail messages. The first one was a group of people talking in the background with someone making a comment to the group about how funny my messages were. The second message was a salesman apologizing for the first message. He said they were having a sales meeting and were looking for new ideas. He had recommended their sales team listen to one of my messages and they forgot to hang up after listening. He also added some of the sales people were going to try it in hopes of growing their sales.

When salespeople are struggling to get customers, let alone getting prospects to return their calls, it sure is nice to have them calling you.

You can have fun in every area of your business. The next two examples are some of the direct marketing packages our company has used for prospecting. The first one was called First Grade. I purchased a tablet of the lined paper like the kind we all used in first grade along with crayons, glitter, and glue – that's right Elmer's glue.

I wrote a short note in crayon on the lined paper saying I had a marketing idea which would help them. Then I sprinkled on glitter and glued a business card to the letter. Finally, I addressed the envelopes in crayon.

You've had prospects who never answer their phone or return messages. I had frequently tried to contact a lady who was like this. Numerous calls and emails to her and not a single response.

The day she got the letter, she called me. The first words out of her mouth were "I had to call the person who would write to me in crayon. Your letter made me laugh."

The other example was a group of prospects in New York City we were marketing to. They were sent a letter package containing pieces of old records. The black vinyl records all of us listened to in the 60's, 70's and 80's. The first line of the letter read "Our clients are breaking records and we want to do the same for you." I then followed up the mailing with a phone call.

Now you have to keep in mind, here I am with my southern accent calling people in New York who have never heard of me or my company. You know the standard response to most prospecting calls like these: "Thank you for calling. Please send me some information about your company that we can keep on file." You might have had a two minute conversation if you were lucky.

When I made my prospecting calls after the letter, not a single person remembered my name or my company until I said I was the guy who sent them the broken records. Then they would suddenly start laughing. After the laughter subsided, we would then start talking about our favorite bands, concerts we had seen and the glory of vinyl. After reminiscing for 20 minutes or more, the person almost always asked me to tell them about my company and how we could help them with marketing.

How many times do you have a potential customer asking you for information about your company?

A word of caution – too much or the wrong kind of humor can cause more harm than good. You've seen the ads on television that are very funny, but you have no idea what product or service is being offered. I bet you can remember your favorite Superbowl ads from the past, but can't remember which company the ad was promoting.

If you're not sure if something is funny, ask someone who will be honest with you. Like the emperor, you want someone who will tell you you're naked. If there is any doubt whether something is funny or proper, don't use it.

Have fun! Rent an old Marx Brothers or Three Stooges movie and have a laugh on me.

Homework Lessons for Success

1. Review your voice mail, away message on your email, brochures and other marketing material. How can you add a little fun to your communications? Change your voice mail message every two weeks. It's very important to keep your messages fresh.

2. Sure Southwest and Disney World can have fun, but not our industry. Wrong!!!! Go to www.wamu.com to see one bank that started having fun and incredible growth. Washington Mutual Bank even started calling itself WaMu. What kind of name is that for a bank?

3. If you need to motivate your team at work, take a lunch hour to watch your favorite comedy and spend a little time laughing.

Lesson 6

Smile

Smile, it's the key that fits the lock of everybody's heart.
~Anthony J. D'Angelo *The College Blue Book*~

Mom always has a smile on her face. Not a goofy grin, but a genuine smile. It's so infectious that the people she meets start smiling too and immediately like her. Mom's smile has been the beginning of many conversations and ultimately friendships. Thankfully, I inherited some of her smile.

It's amazing the positive responses you get from people simply by smiling. A "good morning" coupled with a smile can change someone's entire day - starting with yours. Smiling is a choice just like frowning. I smile all the time - when I meet someone, speak at conferences, order lunch and talk with people over the phone. There is almost always a good reason to smile. It helps you connect with people whether you're talking to a large group or one-on-one.

If you think about it, a smile's effect is universal. It doesn't matter where you're from, your age or the size of your bank account. A smile can change your day.

On a trip to New York City, I was standing in line at the Shake Shack to get one of their awesome cheeseburgers. When the young lady looked up to take my order, she saw my smile and her whole expression changed. She asked me why I looked so happy to which I explained it was a beautiful day and I was about to eat one of the world's best cheeseburgers. She and the other lady at the counter both looked at me and gave me the biggest smile back. She asked me where I was from, thanked me for coming, and invited me to please come back again.

Another lady who filled my order had also noticed my smile and gave me extra fries even though I certainly didn't need them. I wasn't smiling to get extra fries, but more often than not something like this happens.

When you smile and are nice to people, they will in turn want to be nice to you. I had made her day a little better by smiling and she wanted to give me something back in return. This is one of those special bonuses in life that none of us ask for or expect, but is always appreciated.

Try smiling the next time you're on the phone. It will change your whole attitude while talking to a friend or customer. My great friend, Andrea Nierenberg, is also a smiler and an extremely successful author, speaker and trainer. She suggests in her best-selling book, *Million Dollar Networking,* keeping a mirror at your desk to always remind yourself to smile during phone calls. You will quickly see a difference in how people respond to you and how your phone calls just got better.

Hopefully, you can see my smile while you're reading this book. Clients and friends who subscribe to my enewsletter, *Direct Marketing Tips,* tell me they enjoy reading it, because it has valuable marketing information and makes them smile. I try to put a little smile into everything I do.

This is probably why I am a customer and big fan of Southwest Airlines and Disney World. Both companies put a smile in how they do business and I don't think any of us could argue with their success. We all like doing business with people who make us smile.

Southwest recently influenced federal regulations to allow direct flights into Love Field in Dallas. The campaign to get those changes was called Set Love Free. All their ticket agents wore shirts reading Set Love Free and hung banners encouraging their customers to get involved.

There was even a website, www.setlovefree.com, where you could get more information on the campaign and order your own shirts with Set Love Free. With the news of the changes, Southwest had employees dressed like airplanes going to Love Field. The entire campaign had all their passengers smiling including me.

Much of your success in life is based on how you make others feel. Legendary motivator, speaker and trainer, Zig Ziglar, often shares this important piece of wisdom "You can have everything in life you want; if you just help enough other people get what they want."

I mentioned earlier about the Cavalier Shop passing out bottled Cokes from an old style cooler and the two direct marketing packages, First Grade and Breaking Records. The reason both the Cokes and direct marketing packages worked so well was because they reminded the person of a happy time in their life. They made the person think back to the fun of recess in the first grade, of sticking your hand in ice cold water to get a Coke, or of standing in the third row of a Rolling Stones concert watching Mick do his thing.

That brief, simple memory from the past made them smile or laugh. Help people have that feeling and you will be successful.

People want to feel good and a smile is one of the easiest and least costly ways to help them feel that way. You don't need special training, any set of lips will do, and your face won't become permanently stuck while flashing a huge smile. You can even fake a smile at first until you get the hang of it and see how it benefits you and those around you.

If eating ice cream at Ben and Jerry's or going to Disney World can put a smile on your face, then why shouldn't we demand the same kind of experience when getting your driver's license renewed or calling tech support for your computer? I'm not saying the person behind the counter at the Department of Motor Vehicles serve Cherry Garcia when getting your license or the person on the phone talk like Donald Duck. I'm just asking both of them to smile and ask "How may I help you today?" That's not hard.

There are times in life when it's not appropriate to smile, but too many people look for reasons not to smile. Don't be one of them. It takes only 14 muscles to smile and 43 to frown. Worst of all, frowning causes wrinkles and none of us want any more of those.

Tomorrow when you get out of bed, go straight to the mirror and smile. You will feel better about starting the day. Plus, you'll have that first smile out of the way and they just get easier as the day goes.

Go ahead and smile... I know you want to!

Homework Lessons for Success

1. Every morning when you wake up, choose to smile that day.

2. Keep a mirror at your desk to help remind you to smile while you're talking on the phone. I wouldn't recommend a big mirror. Someone might become concerned about your vanity.

3. Have a contest to see how many people's day you can brighten by smiling. Even if it's just one, you are both winners.

Lesson 7

Be Positive

If you look for the positive things in life, you will find them.　　　　　　　*~Author unkown~*

Mom has such a positive outlook on life. She's always looking for the best in everyone. In high school and college, my brothers and I were like a lot of boys...always looking for the prettiest girls to date. Needless to say we were somewhat shallow in our approach to dating.

From time to time, Mom would meet girls our age and suggest to us the ones she thought we might want to go out with.　Amazingly, she has never met an ugly girl. It didn't matter what the girl looked like, Mom would always comment on how pretty and nice she was. Later my brothers and I realized Mom was right. She was looking beyond outward appearances to the kind of person the girl was.

My dad also helped us in this area. When any of us boys would start saying something mean about one of our brothers, and it happened quite often, he would quote Thumper from the movie, Bambi. "If you don't have anything nice to say, don't say anything at all."

This approach to life can be extremely valuable in all your relationships – family, work, and social. When working with a difficult customer, write down several positives about that customer. You begin to look at that customer differently and suddenly it becomes much easier to work with them. Do the same thing for your boss, fellow employees, family members or anyone else with whom you might have a problem.

This doesn't mean you can never be critical of someone's performance, just do it in a positive tone. A little tough love is sometimes needed to help a person get back on track.

Being positive applies not only to looking for the good in people, but how you approach life. How do you respond to the inconveniences that come your way every day?

I recently stopped at a local grocery to pick up an order of chicken for dinner. The lady behind the counter told me they had just run out of chicken and were cooking more. Then she asked if I would mind shopping for 10 minutes and she would have it ready when I came back. I thanked her and said that's great.

After about 15 minutes I went back to the deli to get my chicken. The lady apologized and told me the chicken was still not ready. I told her that was fine and that I didn't mind waiting. We talked about her day and how busy the store was. When the chicken was finally ready, she boxed mine and said she had taken care of me. I thanked her and went on my way not thinking any more about it.

When I opened the box at home, my eight piece order had grown to twelve pieces. Both of our positive attitudes had made the situation so much more enjoyable. If I had gotten mad because it was taking too long, it would not have made a bit of difference in how fast I got my chicken and both of us would have left with a bad attitude. Instead, we were both very happy and my growing boys got four more pieces of chicken to eat.

Again, let me clarify something. Don't have a positive attitude just to get extra chicken breasts. You keep a positive attitude because it's the right thing to do. You will always feel better about any circumstance and so will the other person.

Let me share with you a great example of what I'm talking about. Recently I was on a commuter flight from New York to Birmingham which was scheduled to depart at 4 p.m. Due to a myriad of different problems, our plane was stuck on the runway for hours waiting to take off. As you can imagine, our lone flight attendant was being bombarded with questions, threats, demands and many other issues. I happened to be sitting by her in the very front and watched this all take place.

At one point during our ordeal, she asked me why I wasn't upset like the other passengers. To which I replied that I was comfortable, had plenty of work to do, pretzels to eat and knew there had to be a very good reason why we couldn't leave. I smiled and told her we would all get home eventually. She went on to thank me numerous times for being so positive.

Did I get a free airline ticket, hotel room, or meal for waiting with such a positive attitude? No, after eight hours of sitting on the runway, we came back to the gate and were told our flight would leave the next morning. I got the same thing the guy who was cursing got - nothing. We were told good luck with finding a meal or hotel room at midnight.

I slept on the floor of the airport and finally got something to eat at 6 a.m. when the restaurants opened. Another funny thing about the whole ordeal was that our flight the next morning was delayed one hour because they couldn't find our luggage from the night before.

Being positive didn't get me anything special other than a stressed flight attendant's thanks and a story to tell. And, my mom would tell you that was more than enough.

There is so much negativity in our world. Many people only look for the flaws in others and the bad in everything that happens. To be more successful, start looking for the good in people and in every situation.

There's the story of a teacher who took over a class of what she thought were gifted students. That year her class excelled and at the end of the year the school honored her for this great achievement. It was at that time she realized that her class was actually made up of trouble makers and students who had all been behind in school. Her positive attitude focused on the good in these students and changed their lives. It also taught that teacher a valuable life lesson.

Successful businesses have this same attitude. The cast members at Disney World do a great job of taking a positive approach toward their customers. You can imagine the number of families in any one day whose kids are tired and something goes wrong. The Disney cast always has a positive, can do attitude that wants to solve every family's problem.

During one of our family's early visits to Disney World, we were about to leave for home when one of my boys finally got up enough courage to ride the Tower of Terror. When we reached the ride, the wait time was almost two hours. Being the caring, loving dad I am, I told everyone we couldn't wait that long and needed to be on the road home. Seeing my son's disappointment, I stopped a cast member and explained our problem.

He quickly said not to worry and would see what he could do. Within 10 minutes, my son was at the front of the line and got his last minute chance to scream. Our family was already in love with the whole Disney World experience and this situation illustrated beautifully why we feel that way and keep going back.

Start today looking for the best in everyone and every circumstance. You just may find it.

Homework Lessons for Success

1. How do you handle life's inconveniences? Your dry cleaning is not ready and the movie is sold-out. Sounds like a great excuse to buy a new outfit and change your date plans to coffee and conversation.

2. Let people see your positive attitude. It becomes contagious.

3. Always keep Thumper's motto in mind. "If you don't have anything nice to say, don't say anything at all."

Lesson 8

Keep It Simple

Go confidently in the direction of your dreams!
Live the life you've imagined. As you simplify your
life, the laws of the universe will be simpler.

~*Henry David Thoreau*~

If you haven't figured it out by now, my mom is not a very complicated person. It took her forever to finally try a microwave. The dishwasher at home is either she or Dad. Mom likes to keep her life simple.

It is this simplicity that endears so many people to my mom. They know exactly what they're getting when dealing with Mom. It puts people at ease because they know there are no games being played.

In our ever more complicated world, people from all walks of life are looking for ways to simplify their lives. The more you can do to help them simplify, the more successful you will be.

In all the marketing we do for our clients, one of the key components is simplicity. We try to keep everything very simple like never requiring a customer or prospect to remove a coupon or some other type of reply device with scissors. You've seen the dotted line and the little picture of scissors on something you've received in the mail. They want you to get up, find scissors and cut off the coupon.

I never did well with scissors. Mom always had to correct me for running with scissors and having the blades pointing up. Are you asking your customers to run with scissors?

Some of the best direct mail packages have been a simple black and white letter versus an expensive full color brochure.

If a customer sees your ad and goes to your website wanting to buy your product, be sure the first page they reach gives them the opportunity to purchase your product. Don't send them to a home page and then make them navigate your entire site to finally find the page to make a purchase.

If you need the customer to fill out some information, keep it simple. No matter how great the credit card company makes the offer, none of us want to fill out the long application form on the back of their letter. It's too complicated.

The easier you make it for your customer to make a purchase, or your donor to send a gift, the greater the chance your customer or donor will take the action you desire.

Look at your sales process and ask yourself if it's easy to do business with your organization. When customers call, are they lost in "automation world" holding and listening to option after option? One of the biggest complaints consumers have is getting an automated answering system when they call and the maze of numbers you have to press before you actually talk to a real person. Wouldn't talking to a real live person make it easier for you?

I didn't inherit Mom's ability to keep life simple. I have a laptop computer, answering machine and cell phone that all do more things than I care to know about. Yet despite all of this, I'm constantly working to simplify my life. Keeping things simple is one of the keys to being successful.

Another aspect of simplicity is seeing life as a child. Mom has a special way of looking at things much in the same way a child does. When one of their farm animals has a baby, Mom gets so excited you'd think it was another grandchild. As you grow older, don't lose that awe of the simple things of life - a spring flower, the shape of a cloud or walking barefoot through the grass.

All of you know the words to this classic poem and have probably written or said it at some point in your life:

Roses are red, Violets are Blue,
Sugar is sweet, my love, But not as sweet as you.

Whether you're 8 or 80, you understand the meaning to this poem. The words are simple yet powerful and convey a wonderful message. Do your words have the same effect?

Too many of us complicate our lives and the lives of our customers by trying to sound too sophisticated in our communication. We find the word of the day from our thesaurus and try to impress our customers and colleagues with the big words we know.

It would be facile for me to palaver with you about my voluminous vocabulary which I imbibed while attending Mississippi State University, but none of ya'll are perspicacious enough to decipher my animus.

Your friends are never going to get a dictionary to look up a word you've used. So why do you think your customers or prospects are going to take the time? Take a look at how you're communicating with your customers and ask yourself if what you're saying is simple enough for a twelve-year-old to understand.

Use simple, power words. People are much more interested in buying from you if you have something "FREE" or "New" to show them. Even I can understand those words.

Take this simple approach with all your marketing – TV, radio, direct mail, print ads, websites, brochures – or even your resume. Everyone wants to design a beautiful brochure, ad, direct mail package or commercial. These award winning designs have only one problem - they don't get results.

My experience and other studies have shown simple works very well. A simple design that's easy to read, easy to understand the benefits, and makes it easy to purchase will almost always beat the four color complicated design. Simple is the best approach when marketing your products, services or yourself.

Amazon.com has made it very simple to buy a book and many other products. eBay made it very easy to sell or buy almost anything. You too can be an industry leader like these companies if you find a way to simplify life for your customers. If I'm unable to get in my car and drive to the local bookstore, buying a book is only a click away.

The Gettysburg Address is less than 300 words and took just over two minutes to give. Yet, these simple words are considered one of the greatest speeches in history.

Create some history for yourself by making everyone's life simpler.

Homework Lessons for Success

1. Simplify your life by eliminating unimportant activities. You will automatically be more successful when you decide to focus your efforts. Are you trying to be too many things? Jack Welch, the former leader of GE, decided if GE was not first or second in any business segment that segment was sold. He only wanted to be in the areas where they were the best.

2. Go through your closet and give away the things you haven't worn or used in a year. If you're spending money on storage space for personal items, you might have too much stuff.

3. Start looking at life like a child. Enjoy a puppy licking your face, a beautiful sunrise, and all the other wonders of life that are right in front of you.

Lesson 9

Honesty

No legacy is so rich as honesty.

~William Shakespeare *All's Well that Ends Well*~

My mom makes Abraham Lincoln look like a dishonest person.

I don't think Mom has ever told a lie, unlike her children. This story is a perfect illustration of Mom's honesty. While shopping at Wal-Mart, Mom stopped to put on lipstick. A Wal-Mart associate, someone who had never met Mom (and there aren't many), saw her put the lipstick back in her purse. The associate asked Mom to empty her purse to check for what the lady thought was a stolen item.

Naturally there was nothing there and the lady apologized. Mom felt so bad that her actions had led someone to suspect she had stolen something; she in turn apologized profusely to the lady for what had happened.

Mom also clearly understands what honesty means. Not only does she not lie, but you don't have to read between, under or over the lines when she tells you something. She likes to follow what the Bible says on the subject - "Let your yes be yes and your no be no."

As we mature, we learn how to not tell the truth and at the same time not lie. You don't get the real truth until you ask the right question. Our vocabulary grows and we begin to parse words so the other person may not understand the real meaning of what you're saying. Thankfully, Mom knows the meaning of "is."

My boys have learned how to occasionally tell us half-truths. The scenario might go something like this –

Son: ***Can I go out?***

Dad: ***Have you finished your homework?***

Son: ***I've read everything for English and reviewed History. Can I go?***

Dad: ***Have you done your Algebra?***

Son: ***No, I was going to work on it later.***

You've probably had a similar conversation and realized the danger of going down that path. In business and life, I've discovered honesty is the best policy. If something goes wrong with one of our client's projects, we immediately call our client and tell them we messed up. We then offer solutions as to how we can fix the problem.

I've made some of these calls myself and it's not fun. At worst you risk losing a customer and at best you have someone upset with you. But it is still the right thing to do. Our experience has proven this out time and time again. Clients are never happy when something goes wrong, but they always appreciate someone being honest with them and fixing the problem.

Honesty is also having the courage to tell the emperor he's naked. Our company consults with a lot of organizations on their marketing strategies. Many times when we go in to help develop the strategy, someone in the organization, usually the owner or president, has already developed a marketing idea and wants us to implement it.

Some of these ideas are great and some are not. It's our job to be honest with our clients and tell them their idea probably won't work. We've never lost a client for being honest. In most of these cases, the president or owner is glad the idea wasn't just rubber stamped and someone was honest with them before the idea cost the business a lot of money.

In these cases where someone needs you to be honest, do it in a way that encourages ideas and other alternatives. Remember every idea is someone's baby and nobody thinks they have an ugly baby.

Never hurt the person by putting them down. Many people like to show others how smart they are and use honesty to do it. Have you ever heard someone say in so many words "That was the stupidest idea I've heard." The free flow of ideas just stops. Their idea may not have been the brightest in the world, but you don't want them to feel stupid for suggesting it and discourage them from ever making a suggestion again.

It's the loaded question that has been the downfall of many a husband – "Do these pants make me look fat?" We need to be honest, but not tear down the person in doing so.

There's an old saying: "If you always tell the truth, you never have to remember what you said." My mom always told us, "your lies will find you out", and she was right!

When I told the occasional lie as a teenager, somehow the truth always came out. As I shared in an earlier chapter, there are many benefits to having a lot of friends. Mom benefited from her enormous network of friends by telling them about her children. This created a legion of spies who were constantly reporting on the activities of her children. I quickly learned it was better to be honest.

Another side of honesty is being real. Are you honest about yourself and not a fake?

Mom is one of the most real individuals you will ever meet. There is nothing fake about her. She is just a very genuine person who is never concerned about driving the nicest car, having the latest in fashion or being seen with the "right" people. Those things are just not important to her. She couldn't tell you what kind of car she drives, much less what someone else drives.

Mom understands her strengths and weaknesses. She doesn't feel the need to act like she has all the answers and is comfortable in saying "I don't know" or "I can't do this or that." Because Mom doesn't feel the need to try and impress others, her personality doesn't change based on the people she's around.

Thomas Merton, one of the most influential Catholic authors of the 20th Century, made this distinction between the false self we project to the world and the true self that God knows. He said, "For me to be a saint means for me to be myself."

Mom doesn't try to be someone she's not. She is very comfortable with how God created her and has no desire to be someone else or live their life. This attitude alone can make your life so much better. Life is more fun when you are happy with yourself.

Growing up the oldest of five kids on a small farm, I didn't have a lot of money in high school. Right after getting my drivers license in 1975, I bought a ten-year-old VW Beetle. It had no air conditioning, the heater didn't work and on a good day going downhill it could reach speeds of 55 mph.

A typical date consisted of a romantic meal at McDonalds or Pizza Hut and a movie. Sure it would have been fun to drive a Corvette and have a really nice meal at the Sizzler. But I knew that if a girl went out with me, it was because she liked me. I didn't have any airs to put on and was very comfortable puttering down the road listening to my AM radio.

One of the successful investors of our time, Warren Buffet, lived in the same middle-class neighborhood and drove an older model vehicle for years. That attitude is a part of who Warren Buffet is. It doesn't matter how much money he has. He's honest about who he is. Sam Walton was the same way. He continued driving a pickup truck and visiting his stores long after becoming a billionaire.

As a business owner, you have to be honest about your strengths and weaknesses. If you're not very good on the sales side, hire someone who is and let them do what they do best. If you try to be all things in your business, you will not be very good at any of them. It takes a lot of honest, self-evaluation to realize you don't have to know everything and it's smart business to hire a team that's smarter than you.

You also need to honestly evaluate your business to determine its strengths. Too many companies have gone out of business because they got away from their strengths. Focus on what you do best.

I can not tell a lie. Honesty is the best policy.

Homework Lessons for Success ◯

1. Never tell a lie. Once you start down this path, you usually have to tell multiple lies to keep covering for the previous lie. If you mess up, confess it and make it right.

2. Be honest with yourself about who you are. Life is hard enough without trying to be someone you're not. Stop worrying about keeping up with the Joneses. ◯

3. Do your very best. That's all anyone can ask of you.

◯

Lesson 10

Sacrifice

Dedicate some of your life to others. Your dedication will not be a sacrifice. It will be an exhilarating experience because it is an intense effort applied toward a meaningful end.

~Dr. Thomas Dooley~

Much of our culture sees sacrifice as a bad thing, so having a life that includes sacrifice is not desired by most people. We think about sacrifice in terms of giving up something we really like or deserve.

Mom would offer a much different view.

Mom has always been willing to sacrifice for others. She left her home in New Jersey to move to Mississippi after marrying my dad. I love my home state of Mississippi, but New Jersey to Mississippi in the 1950s - scary. She was obviously in love.

Mom and Dad sacrificed a lot to have 5 kids and send them to college on the income of a small farmer. The list of sacrifices she has made for others is endless, yet Mom would never look at her life as one of sacrifice. Mom wanted to do these things. She willingly moved away for her home to another part of the country. Purposely, she didn't spend much money on herself. Why did she do these things? Not from a sense of sacrifice, but because she loved her husband and kids.

Really successful organizations and people are willing to sacrifice for a greater good. In his book, *Small Giants*, Bo

Burlingham shares the story of eight very successful businesses whose owners gave up growth and more money so they could build a better company to serve their customers.

All the owners of the companies highlighted in his book made a conscience decision to sacrifice a potential future of endless growth and revenues. Instead they created companies that have incredible customer and employee loyalty, industry leading profit margins and are leaders in their community.

Cliff Bar is one of the companies in *Small Giants*. Gary Erickson developed his energy bar in his mother's kitchen and named the company and its product for his father. After eight years, Quaker Oats offered Gary $120 million (over 3 times the company's revenues at the time) to buy Cliff Bar. Gary knew however the company would be moved from its home in Berkley, California to the Midwest and the new management team would totally change the culture.

Minutes before it was time to sign on the dotted line, Gary made a courageous decision to sacrifice a big payoff in order to keep the company in Berkley and continue building something special with his team. It also wasn't an easy decision as he had other investors who wanted their money now. Gary had to go into debt to pay them off.

Incredibly, Gary and his team pulled it off. Cliff Bar's revenues grew the next five years from $39 million to $92 million. But even more importantly to Gary, he kept the quality of the product and his company's culture intact.

The other companies in *Small Giants* all had similar stories. They each sacrificed growth to make their organization better. What sacrifices could you or your organization make to create even more success? And by success I don't necessarily mean more money. Gary Erickson with Cliff Bar did end up with much more money. However, your decision to sacrifice growth might result in less money, but is money all there is? You might judge success by an entirely different set of results – more time with family, less stress, casual office setting, etc.

In 1995 when fire destroyed Malden Mills in Lawrence, Massachusetts two weeks before Christmas, thousands of workers thought their jobs were lost for good. Conventional wisdom was the company would take the insurance money and rebuild elsewhere. The next day the company president, Aaron Feuerstein, announced he would rebuild in Lawrence and keep all the employees on payroll during the reconstruction.

It cost $25 million to keep the employees on payroll and much more than the insurance provided to build a state-of-the-art factory. The resulting debt eventually caused Aaron Feuerstein to lose control of his company. What a sacrifice he made. Yet he did what he knew was right. Feuerstein, a devout Orthodox Jew, explained that he drew on Jewish tradition when faced with a crisis: "When all is moral chaos, this is the time for you to be a mensch," the Yiddish word for an honorable, decent, compassionate person who exceeds justice and strives for righteousness.

Moms and dads are now realizing sacrificing time at work to attend a baseball game, recital or birthday party can create successful kids and families. Some kids and adults alike are sacrificing sodas, donuts, cheeseburgers and ice cream to eat healthy. Others are sacrificing television, video games and spending time online to read, go for walks or have family discussions around the table. All these sacrifices lead to a more successful life.

I would also encourage you to cheat once in a while. Enjoy a big cheeseburger with ice cream for dessert while watching one of your favorite movies. Having a night to splurge a little is okay once in a while. As important as sacrifice is to having a successful life, not forgetting to celebrate your success is just as important.

My four-year-old nephew was going to give up mustard for Lent until my sister reminded him he didn't like mustard. Don't be like him; make your sacrifice count for something.

Homework Lessons for Success

1. Take inventory of every area of your life - work, family, health and spiritual. Then ask yourself are there things you need to give up? Remember some of the things you need to give up are not necessarily bad. You need to replace some of the good things in life with what's best. It's good to take your child to a movie, but it's better to spend time talking.

2. Look at your organization. If you were to have exponential growth, would that be a good thing? Would the culture change? Could you give your customers the level of service they deserve? It may be better to have more controlled growth or stay the same size but raise the level of service. You need to be asking these questions.

3. Don't look at sacrifice as a bad thing. Sacrificing that hour of sleep in the morning to exercise could give you many more nights to sleep.

Lesson 11

Passion

Only passions, great passions, can elevate the soul to great things. ~Denis Diderot~

Mom is very passionate when it comes to caring about people. She truly loves meeting people, learning all about them and helping them if needed. It's this passion that makes her so good at what she does.

Recently, I was very sick with a bacterial infection and lost 15 pounds. Every day, Mom called to check on my progress, called all my siblings to update them, and prayed for me to get well. While I appreciated her concern, I told her it was not life threatening and she didn't need to worry so much. Mom responded that if it had been life threatening, she would have been at my side.

You might be thinking most of us would be passionate about our child being sick, but my mom cares this way about all her friends.

To really be successful, you must be passionate first about people and secondly about what you do. I have never met a truly successful person who didn't love what they were doing.

Widely recognized sales guru, Jeffery Gitomer, puts it this way "Love drives true passion. And passion drives achievement. If you don't love what you do, odds are you will not achieve your goal, let alone your dreams. Why would you put that much energy into something you don't love?"

A lot of so-called successful people talk about being "driven." Don't get driven confused with having passion for what you do. Being driven means something else is in control – insecurity, fear, jealousy, rage, envy, hate, a need to win at all cost, etc. If you're driven to be successful, you probably really don't love what you're doing and are certainly not enjoying the journey.

This scenario is frequently played out in the lives of young people whose parents drive them to be successful in some area of competition – sports, school, and music. A young boy who is taken to baseball lessons weekly and practices daily becomes an all-star shortstop. After years of little league, the young man is burnt out and doesn't even want to play baseball in high school. He was driven to be the best, but didn't really love the game.

Mother Teresa had a real passion for those she served in India. Her words demonstrate this passion so well. "By blood, I am Albanian. By citizenship, an Indian. By faith, I am a Catholic nun. As to my calling, I belong to the world. As to my heart, I belong entirely to the Heart of Jesus." The heart is where your passion lives and why passion and love are so interchangeable. Mother Teresa's love was for the poor of India whom she ministered to for almost 70 years.

I don't think any of us can argue with her success.

We've all met people who were passionate about their work. Of all the things I do, speaking to a group of people is the one thing I am most passionate about. No matter what the size of the audience or the location – Sunday School class, Rotary meetings, national conferences, etc. – I love it.

And believe it or not, organizations actually pay me to speak! I get paid to do something I love. Isn't that great? But here's my dirty little secret - I would speak even if they didn't pay me. There are times when an organization can't afford to pay me and I will speak anyway. If you really love what you're doing, the money is not as important.

(Remember, keep that free speaking stuff just between you and me.)

Homework Lessons for Success

1. What are you passionate about in life? When If you've lost some of the passion in your work, take some time to go back and do the things you really loved when you were new with the company. If you're a sales manager, get in the field and make some calls.

2. Read the biographies of passionate people to get you inspired. Mother Teresa, Martin Luther King, Jr. and Billy Graham are good ones to start with.

Section 3

Actions

We have too many high sounding words, and too few actions that correspond with them.

~ Abigail Adams~

Being a good friend, having a good attitude and becoming successful are best seen in the actions you take. You will never become successful waiting for your ship to come in, because you never sent your ship out. You have to get off the sidelines and into the game.

The Bible says a person is known by their fruits. What kind of fruit are you producing? Take an inventory of your actions. Which ones are taking you closer to being successful and which ones are keeping you stuck in mediocrity?

Lesson 12

Stay
in
Touch

A man should keep his friendships in constant repair.
~*Samuel Johnson*~

Mom constantly stays in touch with her friends. When you call her at night, the line is usually busy. She loves talking with friends on the phone. During the week, Mom travels to one of the neighboring towns for the primary purpose of seeing friends. While she may need to make several stops: the bank, grocery store, etc, each one involves catching up with someone she knows. She stops at Wal-Mart to get a few items and visits with the staff and other customers. She has lunch with a different group of friends each day at a different restaurant (different sets of waitresses to see). She walks the mall not for exercise or shopping, but to see people. Sundays, when church is over, she lingers to visit with everyone.

If you haven't seen my mom recently, you can expect a phone call or a note. Mom sends a lot of notes or cards to let you know she's thinking about you. Depending on your circumstances, you might get a birthday, Christmas, anniversary, graduation, sympathy, congratulations for a new baby or an assortment of other cards. Mom knows what's going on in her friends' and family's lives, and she wants to share that moment with them.

How well do you stay in touch with your customers and prospects? Whatever your approach, look for ways to improve and make every customer feel more like a friend.

A financial investor I've used in the past sends me a birthday card every year with a stick of gum in the card. Hilton Honors program emails me special promotion offers at their properties and new ways to earn points. Last year, I purchased steaks from Omaha Steaks and now I get a call and a letter once a month from them.

I keep note cards and stamped envelopes with me all the time. That way after any important meeting, the first thing I do is write a note and mail it. I've had people from other cities call and thank me for the note they received the day following our meeting. I also write notes to people I meet or hear at conferences, lunches, networking events, and so on. This is a great use of your time when you are waiting for your flight at the airport or on a long flight home.

The key to staying in touch with your customers and prospects is always providing something of value. If you call a customer once a week to say "Hi" and ask when they'll be purchasing your product again, the customer will hate your calls. I have sales people calling me back to ask if I had any projects for them. They are nice people, but I don't look forward to their calls because it's always about them and what I can do for them.

However, if you offer them something of value, they will always be excited to hear from you. The best thing I've found to send a customer is new business. Every organization I know of wants new customers. If you can help them make a connection or send a lead, they will always take your call.

Information is valued by everyone. Send your customer and prospects an article about their industry or ideas on how to make their business better. If you see competitive information or new trends in their industry which may help your customer or prospect, send it with a note, or email the information to them.

Every other month, I send an enewsletter, *Direct Marketing Tips,* to my customers and friends. I consistently get emails back thanking me, telling me how one of the tips helped them and asking me to add others to the distribution list. It has nothing to do with my writing expertise, thankfully. It's because there is something in the newsletter that helped them in their business, gave them an idea or just made them laugh.

If you read an article where someone you know has been promoted, changed jobs, won an award, had a major accomplishment in their life or a member of their family has done something special, send a note congratulating them along with the article. As much as people love accomplishing something, what they really love is being recognized for their accomplishments and those of their family.

Homework Lessons for Success

1. Keep note cards and envelopes with you at all times. Then make good use of any down time you have during the day to write a few notes.

2. Be timely when thanking someone.

3. Develop a system for staying in touch with your customers and prospects. Vary your methods throughout the year - email, letters and phone calls. It is vitally important that every contact include something of value. Don't just call customers or prospects to say "Hi."

Lesson 13

Putting Others First

> ***If anyone wants to be first, he must be the very last, and the servant of all.***   *~Mark 9:35 NIV~*

Putting others first starts from the first time you meet them. One of the main reasons Mom is able to talk to anyone and make friends so easily is that the conversation is never about her. She is interested in the other person.

You've met people who go on and on talking about their life and accomplishments. When at last they stop for a moment to ask you a question, you're thinking finally it's my turn. Then the person asks what you think about their life and starts talking again.

How interested are you in the other person and putting them first? Here are four steps to putting someone first while talking to them.

First ask questions. Many of us believe the people who are easy to talk to and great conversationalist are the ones who know a lot of big words and can talk endlessly. Mom proves just the opposite, that anyone one can do this just by asking questions.

You might be thinking you can't talk to people the way my mom does. You never know what to say. Don't worry, that's a good thing. Instead of thinking of something to say, ask questions. Mom will say hello to someone and start asking them questions about their life. Where are you from? Do you have children or grandchildren? And with every answer there is a new question.

These are just a few of the questions you can ask. Even if you know nothing about their answer, you can still ask a follow up question. Let me show you what I mean.

You: *What do you do for a living?*

New friend: *Astrophysics*

You: *Astrophysics. Wow, that sounds really interesting. Tell me more about it.*

Try to avoid asking questions that can be answered with yes/no or one word. If your question does have a one word answer, ask a follow up question like the above example. Before the person knows it they've spent thirty minutes sharing about their life and you've made a new best friend.

The second step in being easy to talk to is listening. Very few people really listen these days. You are trying to think about what you are going to say next. Listening is work and you have to practice it. One way to show people you're listening is to repeat what the person said and ask them if what you said is correct.

Mom will nod her head, smile and encourage the person to keep talking. When she is asked about her family, Mom tells about her 5 children and 12 grandchildren and then turns the conversation back to the other person.

The third step is to look the person in the eye and be in the moment. How many times have you been talking to someone and thinking about something totally different? Putting the other person first is listening to every word they say and not thinking about your plans for lunch.

In addition to our minds being somewhere else, you can be guilty of constantly looking over the person's shoulder to see who else is in the room. When you're talking to someone, your total focus should be on them.

The fourth step is Mom never feels the need to outdo the other person. She is not trying to interrupt and tell her story. Many of us can't wait for the other person to finish their story, so we can share a better one. If someone is telling you about the hole-in-one they made in golf, you are immediately ready to tell about your hole-in-one playing with Tiger Woods. Instead you should follow Mom's example and repeat what you were told along with a positive comment. "You made a hole-in-one. Wow, that's great."

These concepts also apply when you are marketing your company or yourselves to others. I see so many ads, direct mail pieces, commercials and other marketing pieces that are focused on the company and what it does instead of how it can help its customers. How many ads start with how long the company has been in business, how big the warehouse or store is, or showing a long list of equipment the company has? Customers don't care. They are only interested in how you are going to make their life better.

Putting your customer first can be seen in how your product or service is designed, manufactured, marketed and used. Mac computers were designed with the user in mind.

Macs were the first computers to come in different colors. The other manufacturers never thought someone might like their computer in a different color. Disney World first designed its Fast Pass program to make things better for their guests. A Fast Pass allows you to skip the long lines and go to the front if you return to the ride at a certain time. Now Fast Pass users don't have to wait in line and Disney World can better manage traffic flow at its rides.

Putting your customer first also means not being so rigid with your company policy unless it's that the customer comes first. How many of you have asked a simple request of some store and the customer service person says "Sorry, I can't help you. It's company policy." The policy was designed to make things easier for the company, not to better serve the customer.

Look around at what you and your company are doing to put your customers and friends first. If you have your priorities backwards, take a cue from Mom and start making everyone feel special.

Homework Lessons for Success

1. Are your conversations about you or the other person? People like to talk about themselves, so let them. You will be their best friend.

2. Review all your company policies. Do they help or hurt your customer? If it hurts the customer or makes their experience less than incredible, stop it.

3. Let others have their time in the spotlight. Allow your customers, coworkers, spouse, children, friends or whoever it may be to have center stage. There's a story of a woman who met Rene Descartes and another famous person of that time. The other man made her feel like he was the most important person in the room. Rene Descartes made her feel like she was the most important person in the room.

Lesson 14

Give

Unto

Others

That's what I consider true generosity. You give your all, and yet you always feel as if it costs you nothing.   ~Simone de Beauvoir~

Mom loves giving gifts. Birthday, anniversary, graduation, Christmas, baby showers or a "little happy" as she calls it to let you know she was thinking about you. Mom also gives to people who are going through a struggle in life. It may be financial, physical or some other kind of challenge. We know she does this from some of the people she's helped in the past who thanked us for her help. Mom never tells us she's doing it or who she's helping.

Growing up on a small farm, our family didn't have a lot of money, but Mom helped people however she could. With five children and the first four boys, we were always out growing clothes. Mom would gather everything that wouldn't fit one of us and we would take it to another family who needed them. All of us learned the importance giving to others from watching Mom.

Now, I try to do the same thing at my company. When a new client comes on board, we might send a King Cake, the wonderful pastries made famous at New Orleans Madri Gras. The note will say we're celebrating having them as a client. In addition to sending a gift for special events in our clients' lives, our customer service and sales people know they can take cookies, donuts, cakes, or any other goodie to our clients for no other reason than to say "Thank You."

We want our clients to feel special and have our gifts standout. Years ago, when we were a very small company, I realized we didn't have the money to compete with the Christmas gifts some of our competitors were giving. We couldn't afford expensive gift baskets for our clients, yet I wanted our gift to be special.

Kathie, my wife and the other amazing woman in my life, offered to make Christmas candy. Since 1993, she has made wonderful homemade candy which we pack in beautiful Christmas tins and trays. Needless to say our clients loved the candy, and we hit a home run. What our clients really liked in addition to the candy's great taste was the personal effort Kathie had made. They had gotten a homemade gift made by the boss's wife.

Now, I am asked every year by clients if Kathie is making the candy again. It's become an annual tradition that our clients look forward to and love telling others about.

You might be thinking to yourself, how can I make homemade candy for the thousands of customers our company serves? One answer might be to partner with a company like Mrs. Fields Cookies and send one of their coupons to all your customers. The key is to be creative. People love getting gifts, so find ways you can make your customers, friends and family feel special.

The same philosophies apply outside of work. Rick Warren, author of the bestseller *A Purpose Driven Life*, said there's nothing wrong with making a lot of money. The sin is dying with a lot of money. I heard another wealthy person say of his philosophy on giving money from their family foundation, "When I die, I want the last check to bounce because I've given it all away."

We should want to give our time and our dollars to individuals and organizations that need it the most. Warren Buffet recently announced he is giving over $30 billion dollars to Bill Gates' charitable foundation.

Famed industrialist Andrew Carnegie said it this way "The day is not far distant when the man who dies leaving behind him millions of available wealth, which was free for him to administer during life, will pass away unwept, unhonored, and unsung, no matter to what uses he leaves the dross which he cannot take with him. Of such as these the public verdict will then be: 'The man who dies thus rich dies disgraced.'" Carnegie spent the first half of his life making money and the second half giving it away.

Please don't think that only millionaires and billionaires have the ability to give to others. The examples of Mom and Mother Teresa show everyone has the ability to give regardless of the size of their bank account.

Hopefully you're not one of those people who believes there is a fixed amount of ideas, resources and money. If you share any of what you have, it's lost forever. New ideas and wealth are being created all the time. I send my enewsletter, *Direct Marketing Tips*, to anyone who asks to receive it, which some people think is crazy. What if a competitor steals your ideas? My answer has always been the same – many of my best ideas were taking someone else's work and building upon it. Sharing my ideas with others has only helped me, never hurt.

Is it time, money or something else? Take a moment today to consider what you can share or who you can help.

P.S. Don't feel too bad for Kathie. While it is hard work, she's paid very well for her labor of love.

Homework Lessons for Success

1. Find new fun gifts to send your friends. King Cakes can be ordered at 1-800-442-1342 or go online at www.haydelbakery.com.

2. Believe it or not, here are some recipes I want to share with you:

CANDY RECIPES

Peanut Butter Roll

Ingredients: 1 stick of butter, 1 lb. box of powdered sugar, creamy peanut butter, 1 tsp. of vanilla, 5 tsp. Pet milk

Mix butter (not softened), powdered sugar and Pet milk in a mixing bowl. It will look dry. Add vanilla. You may need to add more powdered sugar until it is a good consistency to roll out on wax paper without sticking. Roll flat and spread peanut butter all over. Roll into a log and wrap in wax paper. Place in refrigerator overnight. Slice and serve.

Homework Lessons for Success

(Continued)

Chocolate Clusters

Ingredients: 12 oz. each of butterscotch and chocolate chips, 3 cups of salted peanuts.

Melt the butterscotch and chocolate chips in a double boiler. Add peanuts, mix and drop by spoonfuls onto wax paper to cool and harden. May add paraffin if needed.

Haystacks

Ingredients: 12 oz. Butterscotch chips, 16 oz each of chow mien noodles and salted peanuts.

Melt butterscotch chips in double boiler. Add peanuts and noodles, mix and drop by spoonfuls onto wax paper to cool and harden. May add paraffin if needed.

3. The more creative you can be with your gift the more the other person will love the gift. It shows you cared enough to spend time thinking about it.

Lesson 15

Mind Your Manners

Good manners will open doors that the best education cannot. ~Clarence Thomas~

Growing up, my brothers and I knew one of the fastest ways to get in trouble with Mom was to be impolite or disrespectful. While my mom was from another part of country, she quickly expected her children to adopt the Southern tradition of "Yes ma'am" and "No ma'am."

I remember visiting my grandparents in New Jersey and all my grandmother's friends telling me how nice it was that I said "Yes ma'am." They also thought my accent was cute, but that's another story. Mom taught all her children to be respectful to everyone regardless of sex, race, religion, age or ethnic background.

Good manners have been forgotten to a large degree in our society today. People no longer have respect for one another. Look at how men and women treat each other now. Women are sometimes surprised when a man holds a door for them or waits in the elevator until they leave first.

Look at the sad state of our political process and the lack of manners and civility. It's a good thing these men and women aren't around my mom. She would have washed out their mouths with soap multiple times.

One of the first things she taught her kids to say was "Thank you." If someone does something for you, you always

107

tell them thank you. Everyone deserves a thank you - your waitress, cashier, bank teller, mechanic, teacher, coach and so on. How good are you at saying "Thank you?"

Have you ever seen those commercials where the person accidentally says something wrong like "Are you pregnant?" to a lady who isn't. The person always recovers by immediately saying "Thank you." The lady smiles and says "You're welcome." As the commercial illustrates, those two simple words can have an amazing effect on people.

We don't thank our customers, supporters, employees and vendors nearly enough. As a customer, I know how it makes me feel when someone thanks me for my business. I am always much more likely to do business with that person again.

The ladies who work at the salon where I get my hair cut do a great job of saying thank you. They are constantly thanking me for being a customer. I am even given a shirt with the word "Guest" on the front to wear during my haircut. It makes me feel special and want to come back.

Going hand in hand with saying "Thank You" is "Please." These truly are the magic words – please and thank you. Mom taught us to say please for any request we had. In turn people respond much faster and are nicer when you say please. In their book, *The Power of Nice*, Linda Kaplan Thaler and Robin Koval share how being nice is the key to being successful in business. It starts with saying please if you want something.

Asking please applies as much to the boss as it does to the

workers. As the boss, you can tell your employees what to do and in most cases they have to do it in order to keep their job. Successful leaders ask people to do something and include a please. In both cases the work gets done, but the boss who asks please has employees who want to do the work and will give their best effort.

Another aspect of good manners she emphasized to us was to say "Hello" when meeting someone. Little boys can get preoccupied with other things when their mother meets someone on the street, but we were taught to look the person in the eye and say "Hello." If it was a man, we would shake hands.

How many of us are guilty of walking up to someone and immediately start asking for something before ever saying "Hello" to the person? In our fast paced life, we have to remember the man or woman across the counter is a person too. We have become so accustomed to our computers giving us instant responses without any personal interaction that we many times expect the same from individuals.

Not if you're with my mom. She taught us there is plenty of time to get your questions answered after you've greeted the person, learned their name and asked them about their day.

You will be much more successful in every walk of life if you show a little interest in people. Saying hello to someone and calling them by their name doesn't cost you anything. Yet it may have a profound effect on the man or woman whose job or life might have beaten them down that day.

Aretha Franklin had it right when she sang about RESPECT. People deserve to be treated with respect, and one of the fastest ways to get a spanking from my mom, not that my brothers or I ever needed one, was to be disrespectful to someone.

Honor and respect are really the same word. It's interesting that only one of the Ten Commandments comes with a promise. Honor your mother and father so that you may live a long life. Honor is a very important part of many eastern cultures - honoring parents and others in authority. You don't have to agree with everything your parents or others in authority say, but you do need to be respectful of their position. This is the same for your manager at work and your spouse at home.

There needs to be a lot more love and respect at home - husbands and wives showing respect to one another. Life is hard enough without alienating your partner. Children need to respect their parents.

How respectful are you of your customers? Their time? When you call someone, do you ask them "Is this a good time for you or is there a better time for me to call back?"

The same is true of emails. You need to get your prospects' and customers' permission to contact them. This next question is even more important. When you do contact customers or prospects via email, phone or mail, do you bring something of value or are you just wasting their time?

How many of you have called or emailed a customer after sending a quote or proposal to ask if they got it? Or have you called to ask a customer if they had any new projects for you? Calling a customer or prospect every month just to say hello and check in is wasting their time.

Instead, why not call the customer to let them know how part of your proposal will save them money or increase sales. Send them ideas to improve their business. If you're doing these things, customers will welcome your calls and emails.

Despite being almost 50, I still say "Yes Ma'am" and "No Ma'am" to older adults. It's not because I'm worried about getting on my mother's bad side or her getting on my back side. Instead, Mom taught me people always deserve to be treated with respect no matter what their status in life. It's a great lesson I hope I never forget.

Now mind your manners. Mom's watching!

Homework Lessons for Success

1. How are you doing in regard to minding your manners? Start with the simple ones - Please and Thank You - then go from there. Hold the door open or give your seat up on the subway for a lady, senior citizen or just anyone who looks tired.

2. Keep a bar of soap near by. The next time you say something you shouldn't have said or have a smart mouth, have a little taste of the soap. It's a great reminder to have good manners.

3. There's no age when it's okay not to mind your manners. Whether you're 7 or 77, you should always be respectful to those around you.

Lesson 16

Keep
Your
Word

The woods are lovely, dark, and deep,
But I have promises to keep,
And miles to go before I sleep,
And miles to go before I sleep.

~Robert Frost~
Stopping by Woods on a Snowy Evening

Mom always keeps her promises. If you say you're going to do something, then do it. As young boys are apt to do, we would promise something and then try to get out of it when a better offer came along or things started getting difficult.

I once agreed to help one of our neighbors with milking his cows, which I'm sure many of you have had the opportunity to do in your lifetime. After 2 days of waking at 5:00 a.m., I knew milking cows was not my thing and didn't want to go back. Mom however reminded me I had promised I would help him for a month until he could find another worker.

We are constantly reminding everyone at our company about the importance of doing what you promised, plus some. If we tell a client their project is mailing on Friday, we do whatever it takes to mail it on Friday even if it costs us extra. We also include a money back guarantee in our marketing. Before someone will invest in you, they want to know you will keep your promises.

Part of the success of Oreck Vacuum Cleaners is their guarantee. If you're not completely satisfied, you get your money back. These days everyone is skeptical and wants some kind of guarantee before they will give you their money.

Be careful not to bait and switch your clients using a guarantee. I received a mailing from a national lawn care company that offered a very good guarantee. The problem was the dreaded asterisk (*) at the end of the sentence. In small print at the bottom of the postcard was a sentence saying the guarantee may not be available at all locations. Why offer a guarantee if it's not available for everyone?

A lot of us are hesitant about offering a guarantee because we're worried someone will take advantage of us. They will use our product for a while and return it for no reason. Fortunately this only occurs a small fraction of the time. The vast majority of people are honest and don't really want to take the time to return it regardless of how well the product is working.

No matter what your product or service, you can offer a guarantee. It reminds customers that you will keep your promises.

Another aspect of keeping your promise is keeping your commitments in life.

Mom and Dad have been celebrating life together for over 50 years. Starting married life 1,600 miles from home, living on a small farm in Mississippi, raising five children (the first four boys and all born in a five year span), and sending their children to college on a limited budget, was tough. It would have been easy to give up, but my mom and dad were committed to seeing it through. Mom was committed to her husband, children and faith.

Why do so many of us have such a great fear of making commitments in life and keeping them? Marriage, job, friends and children are just a few areas where we're afraid to make a commitment. Our world is full of people who are ready to change spouses, jobs, friends, or morals at the slightest little pain.

When the road gets a little bumpy, we're ready to make a change. But, you will never achieve any level of success in life if you are not willing to commit your best no matter how hard it gets. Going forward, you need to ask yourself why you're making a change. Is it to relieve some pain or because it is the best thing for you, your family or your organization?

One of the most powerful examples of commitment is the story of Robert McQuilken, former president of Columbia Bible College. While under his leadership, the college became recognized as one of the premier Christian institutions in training young people for service around the world. He had led the college for 22 years until it was discovered his wife had Alzheimer's.

When Mr. McQuilken resigned as president to care for his wife, there were many people who questioned his decision. One group reasoned that anyone could care for his wife especially since she didn't recognize him any longer, but not anyone could lead the college. The other group asked how he could walk away from God's call for his life.

Mr. McQuilken's responses were magnificent and tell us everything about real commitment. To the group who said his wife no longer even recognizes him, he readily admitted that his wife didn't always know who he was. But that wasn't the point, he told them. The really important thing was that he still knew who she was and furthermore, he let them know that he recognized in her now-forgetful self the same lovely woman he had married those many years ago.

To the group who thought he was walking away from God's call in his life, his words were even more profound - "There is only one thing more important than a calling. And that is a promise. And I promised to be there for her 'til death do us part."

Mr. McQuilken's commitment to his wife grew deeper as their situation became more difficult. How do you react when keeping your commitments becomes harder? I hope you will follow his example of how to be a real success in life.

Is it getting harder to keep your commitments? Don't give up. There are a lot of us out there pulling for you.

Or as an old little league coach told me once when I got hit and wanted to come out "Rub some dirt on it. You'll be fine."

Homework Lessons for Success

○

1. You can't change your past or know your future. You can only commit today to be your best.

2. Every commitment in life worth having comes with some difficulty. As you face difficulties in keeping your commitments, allow the pain to help you grow stronger in your commitment.

○

3. Give your customers a guarantee. It will make you a better company.

○

Lesson 17

Believe

A man is what he believes.   *~Anton Chekhov~*

To be successful, you have to believe in something. First and foremost, my mom believes in God. Her faith in God is the driving force behind all she does in life and her success. It's her foundation in good times and bad. Secondly, she believes in people. You can see it in how she interacts with others.

Despite how bad we were as kids, Mom has always believed in her children. She continues to this day telling me how much she believes in me and how proud she is of me as a husband, father, brother and business owner. You can't know what a powerful motivation this is for me. Knowing someone believes in me makes me want to do my very best in all areas of my life.

What do you believe in – family, government, religion, job, coworkers, friends, favorite sports team, an idea, or yourself? To achieve any amount of real success in life, one of the things you will have to believe in is people. I'm not saying they will never let you down. I guarantee it. You will often be let down by the people in your life, but you still have to believe in them. We can't make it in this life alone.

Parents have to believe in their children. When a child is learning to walk, they are going to fall down again and again. After the child falls, a parent doesn't tell their child I don't believe you will ever walk. The parent picks them up, encourages them and even takes them by the hand as they take those first steps.

A teenager is going to make bad decisions. A good parent helps their teenager learn from those decisions, so they will make better ones the next time.

If you're a manager, you have to believe in your people. They are going to fall down and make bad decisions, but that's how they'll get better. If you think you are the only person who has all the right answers and you don't need to involve others in decisions, you will never reach your full potential.

Just as Mom is always telling me how much she believes in me, it's important for you to tell your employees how much you believe in them. Show how much you believe in your employees by giving them more responsibility and the freedom to make mistakes. You'll be surprised by how hard they'll work not to disappoint your belief in them and to prove their ability to handle new responsibilities.

Earlier in the book I shared the story of Aaron Feuerstein who believed in his employees so much he kept them on payroll after a fire had destroyed his factory. He paid out $25 million while the factory was being rebuilt.

In a 2005 interview with *Fast Company*, Jeff Immelt, CEO of General Electric, shared some of the beliefs that have helped him be a successful leader. "I'm an optimist. I've always believed the future is going to be better than the past.

And I also believe I have a role in that. The great thing about human beings, myself in particular, is that I can change. I can do better. If you can get up every day, stay optimistic, and believe the future is better than the past, those few things get you through a lot of tough times."

There's an old saying that goes "If you don't stand for something, you'll fall for anything." We can replace "stand for" with "believe in." If you don't believe in something, you'll fall for anything.

What is your "something?"

If you don't really believe in what you're selling, making, building, designing, growing or leading, you'll never be a success. The most successful salespeople are those who truly believe their product can make a difference for their customers.

The same is true if you're a leader in your organization. You must believe in your organization and the people you're leading. If not, your leadership will be ineffective.

If you've read this far, I believe in you. You have what it takes. Now keep reading.

Homework Lessons for Success

1. Do an assessment of your life to see where your beliefs lie. Then ask yourself if the foundations of your life are built upon sand or rock. My experience has been the rock wins out every time.

2. If you believe in someone or a group of people, tell them. They will do their best to live up to it. And even if they fail, keep believing in them.

3. The Wright brothers had to believe an airplane could fly. Sam Walton believed there was a better way to sell goods to the public. Walt Disney believed there was a better way to entertain the children and adults alike. You will never do anything great if you don't believe it.

Lesson 18

Recharge

We must always change, renew, rejuvenate ourselves; otherwise we harden.

~*Johann Wolfgang von Goethe*~

Raising five children was especially tough when you have four boys with only a five year age range from oldest to youngest. I'm not sure Mom and Dad really put a lot of thought into that plan. However, Mom did understand the importance of setting aside time to recharge her battery in order to make it through the day.

Really successful people also know when it's time to recharge their batteries before they burn out. You have to look at three areas to recharge – physically, spiritually and emotionally.

Every day after lunch Mom would put the younger ones down for a nap and lock the older ones, of which I was the oldest, out of the house. Don't worry. We lived on a farm and my dad was nearby working. Plus, we could always knock on the door, but it had better be a matter of life or death.

During this time, Mom would kneel by her bed and pray. Those prayers were for her children, husband and strength to get through the day. It was these prayers which recharged her spiritually. Then she would take a short nap to recharge physically.

Mom must have known what she was doing. In an issue of the magazine, *Selling Power,* a study highlights the importance of napping in the performance of sports players, Olympic athletes, and elite runners. But napping is just not for athletes. The study also showed naps helped musicians, scientists and authors perform at their best.

Mom was also right on prayer. Studies have shown the power of prayer and how people who pray live longer. How are you charging your spiritual battery?

Every Wednesday was town day for Mom. She would hire someone to watch us and go into town to buy groceries for the next seven days. The town was only twenty miles away, but Mom left at 8:00am and returned at 5:00pm. This was her time to recharge emotionally. She would have lunch with friends and visit with adults everywhere she went. At the end of the day when she returned home, Mom was ready to face another attack by her wild boys.

How are your spiritual, emotional and physical batteries? Are they running low? If your battery is low, don't feel bad. Everyone needs recharging from time to time. Your job is to find ways to recharge.

In Stephen Covey's best selling book, *Seven Habits of Highly Successful People*, he talks about the importance of "sharpening the saw". Too many of us believe we can work at a fever pitch day after day and our performance will never be affected. Just as a saw needs to be sharpened to stay effective, you too have to take time and stop what you're doing.

If we never stop to sharpen our saw, we might be working hard every day, but accomplishing nothing just the way a dull saw will never cut wood no matter how hard you work.

Skip lunch and go for a walk by yourself. Spend a day at the spa. Sit in the park one afternoon and just watch the clouds. Take a vacation.

When you take your vacation, it's important that you allow some flexibility so every minute is not planned out. Your goal is to relax, be surprised and enjoy the moment.

I would have written something funny here, but needed a nap and a little recharging.

Homework Lessons for Success

1. Do what successful people around the world do - take an afternoon nap. Keep your nap to an hour or less and you'll be amazed how refreshed you'll feel and ready to do more work.

2. Slow down and take an evaluation of your batteries. Where are you running low-physically, emotionally, mentally or spiritually? Develop a plan to get recharged.

3. When you're recharging, PDAs, cell phones, laptops and connections to work are a no-no. You will never be able to clear your head of work and return refreshed, if you are constantly in touch with the office.

Lesson 19

Celebrate

How important it is for us to recognize and celebrate our heroes and she-roes! ~*Maya Angelou*~

Mom and her friends are always looking for a reason to celebrate. If someone has a birthday, a baby, anniversary or any other positive event in their life, Mom is ready to have lunch and celebrate with them. Mom loves giving thanks for all the good things of life.

There's a *Seinfeld* episode where everyday someone at Elaine's office brings a cake to celebrate an event in one of her fellow employees' lives. Initially she thinks having so many celebrations is stupid and vows not to participate. Later she realizes how much she enjoyed the celebrations or at least the cake.

We don't celebrate enough in our life. Lose weight, run a marathon, get a promotion, A's or B's on the report card, chosen for the dance or basketball team, complete a project at work; the list of reasons to celebrate life is endless.

In an earlier section we talked about the importance of sacrifice, giving up good or bad things in our life for the best. Ice cream and cheeseburgers are great, but we don't need to eat them all the time. Our diets should include more fruits and vegetables. Watching a little TV is okay, but we don't need to become couch potatoes. Books and conversation are much better for us. To accomplish something worthwhile in life it is going to take sacrifice. When I was training for the Chicago Marathon, I gave up a lot of the foods I liked and trained hard. However, when I reached certain training milestones, I would celebrate with a pizza, coke and dessert. Then I was back on my training.

It's vitally important to celebrate the milestones, accomplishments, and good things in life. It reminds you that the sacrifices were worth it and makes you thankful for all you've been blessed with in life.

Once a month, we have a luncheon for all our employees. We thank them and remind them of all the great work they've done over the past month. Our business is very fast paced with constant deadlines. You complete one project, catch your breath and the next deadline has started. It's really easy to forget all that's been accomplished and feel like a client doesn't appreciate all you've done.

That's why we celebrate. You should do the same thing at your company.

Celebrations aren't just for the office. Kathie and I try to celebrate at home as much as possible. Every week we have a date to celebrate our wonderful marriage. Our dates are special times we both look forward to, so very seldom do we ever go to a movie on our date night. Usually we have a nice dinner and talk about all that happened in our week. It helps us realize how blessed we are.

You also need to celebrate with your children. Having one son in high school and another in middle school, you quickly see how much pressure they are under and how life is beating them down. A perfect example is my oldest son who got a car shortly after turning 16 and had his first wreck within a week. Thankfully, no one was hurt and there was only limited damage.

As you can imagine, he was devastated and embarrassed. We talked to him about what happened and lessons to learn from the experience. Then we celebrated at dinner that night the fact he and the other person were safe and his car was not damaged.

We've even celebrated a clean room, which is quite a feat.

Celebrations should also remind us that we can't accomplish anything without the help of others. I would have never completed the Chicago marathon without my running partner, Don Steen. We were accountable to each other to meet in the mornings at 4:30 to train. We constantly encouraged each other during the marathon and ran faster that day because of it. That night we celebrated our awesome accomplishment together.

Every promotion or award I've ever received was because of a lot people who helped me and the celebration was about everyone involved.

Have fun and celebrate something.

Homework Lessons for Success

1. Celebrate the successes in your life - big and small. Please keep in mind these celebrations don't have to be mega events. The important thing is the celebration, not the size of the cake. Mom kept one big candle she used over and over again on our birthday cakes. It never once affected the taste.

2. When you're celebrating, be sure to include the people along the way who helped you be successful. A teacher, coach, mentor, the list is endless. I always like to hear the stories of successful athletes who get their first big check and buy their parents a new home.

3. Have a way to remember the special milestones in your life. The Old Testament has numerous examples of the Israelites building a rock altar to remind them of God's miracle and the place it happened.

Last Thought

It's time for reflection. Take a moment now to evaluate your life. How are you doing? Keep in mind success is not reaching a destination, but how you're doing along the way. You never reach a magic number of friends in life and stop making new ones. You don't smile at the first 500 people you meet and then stop smiling. You don't stop celebrating birthdays after 60.

You might be making great progress on your success journey and only need to sharpen up on a few of the lessons I've shared. Others might feel like they've totally blown it and success is just not an option for them. Don't believe it. The past is behind you and even if you have only one more day on this earth, you can be a success. You were created with incredible gifts and now's your chance to use them.

Start today by making a new friend, smiling at someone who's having it rough, thanking someone for how they've helped you and sending a note to an old friend. You will have your first of many successful days.

Mom doesn't have extraordinary looks or intellect. Her name is little known outside of the community where she lives, but her success is unparalleled. I pray that Mom's funeral is many years away, but when the time comes, there won't be a church large enough to hold all the lives she has touched.

My desire is that you have that same kind of success and it starts by learning the lessons of a mama's boy.